イービーティージー EVERYT
BUT THE GIRL
WALKING WOUNDED

Wise Publications
London/New York/Sydney/Paris/Copenhagen/Madrid

イービーティージー

Before Today. I don't want excuses. I don't want your smiles. I don't want to feel like we're apart a thousand miles. I don't want your attitude. I don't want your things. But I don't want a phone that never rings. I want your love and I want it now. I don't want your history. I don't want that stuff. I want you to shut your mouth. That would be enough. I don't care if you've been here before. You don't understand - tonight I feel above the law, I'm coming in to land. I want your love and I want it now. My heart is that much harder now. That's what I thought before today. My heart is that much harder now. I thought that it would stay that way, before today. But I don't want a phone that never rings. I want your love and I want it now.

Wrong. I wanted everything for a little while. Why shouldn't I? I wanted to know what it was like. But I pushed you too far and you started laying down the law till I didn't love you any more. Now you can pull a little bit, there's a little give and take. And love will stretch a little bit but finally it's gonna break. Wherever you go I will follow you, cause I was wrong. So there we both were in that little house just hanging out. You didn't know what you were about. You turned to me as you were threading daisies on a chain and you said - "It's decision time again." Now you can pull a little bit, there's a little give and take. And love will stretch a little bit but finally it's gonna break. Wherever you go I will follow you, cause I was wrong. And the ground's gonna swallow you. I wanted everything for a little while. Why shouldn't I? I wanted to know what he was like. Now you can pull a little bit, there's a little give and take. And love will stretch a little bit but finally it's gonna break. Wherever you go I will follow you, cause I was wrong.

Single. I called you from the hotel phone. I haven't dialled this code before. I'm sleeping later, waking later, I'm eating less and thinking more. And how am I without you? Am I more myself or less myself? I feel younger, louder. Like I don't always connect. Like I don't ever connect. Do you like being single? Do you want me back, do you want me back? Do I like being single? Am I coming back, am I coming back? I'll put my suitcase here for now, I'll turn the TV to the bed, but if no-one calls and I don't speak all day, do I disappear? Look at me without you, I'm quite proud of myself, I feel reckless, clumsy. Like I'm making a mistake, a really big mistake. Now I know, each time I go, I don't really know what I think I know. Do you want me back, do you want me back?

The Heart Remains A Child. I dreamed about you again last night You never have the same face twice, but I always know it's you, and you'r always looking better than you really do. And I walk around the whol next day feeling like I still got something to say. But I don't know what it is and I don't know how to reach you even if I did. Do I wanna hear tha you forgive me? Do I wanna hear you're no good without me? Am I bi enough to hear that you never even think about me? Why should you eve think about me? I thought that I'd outgrow this kind of thing. Tell me, aren' we supposed to mature or something? I haven't found that yet, is this a grown-up as we ever get? Maybe this is as good as it gets. Years may go b but I think the heart remains a child. The mind may grow wise, but the hea just sulks and it whines and remains a child. Why don't you love m Why don't you love me?

Walking Wounded. Out amongst the walking wounded, eve face on every bus is you and me and him and her. Nothing can replace th us I knew. Nothing can replace the us I knew. I'm never gonna let you g You know I'm never gonna let you go. Now I know I had a choice, thoug you never made it clear to me. I thought you never felt it deeply. And nc I'm never gonna let you go. I could have loved you for ever. I could ha loved you for ever. What do you want from me? Are you trying to punish m Punish me for loving you? Punish me for giving to you? Punish me f nothing I do. Punish me for nothing. For nothing. Out amongst the walki

wounded, every face on every bus is you and me and him and her. Nothing can replace the us I knew. Nothing can replace the us I knew. I could have oved you for ever. Or I could have left you for ever. Out amongst the walking wounded, every face on every train is you and me and him and her. Somedays I think I could go insane. Somedays I think I could go insane.

lipside. London, Summer 92 - I think I've changed a lot since then, o you? Ideas that I'd held for years, emotional baggage, hopes and fears, een somehow in a different light, not as wrong, but not as right as they eemed before. Was I different then? Have I changed? And will I change gain? I'm thinking of a mental free-fall, a partial total memory recall like hat of the future, what of the past, what of the present will last? And say I d forget and revert to the old ways, forget this hurt, am I better off or in everse, untaught by experience and therefore worse? I mean a lot. I mean a ttle. I'm like a coastline, a beach and spit - Spurn Point and the rest of it. he sea, the tide, the salt and foam, I'm the blasted land, the sand shifting, ifting out and back, then breached, drowned, defences down, rebuilt from is day on. Or maybe not, maybe my moment's gone. I mean a lot. I mean little. Am I the same person I seemed to be? Does all of this depress me? I on't listen, I won't talk. A weightless life, I moonwalk. I mean a lot. I mean little. I'm supple, brittle, pig in the middle. There's resilience inside my ce, but sometimes nothing. Deep space. What I feel and what I fear is ways here - my atmosphere.

g Deal. You don't know what's wrong, you only know it isn't right. u don't remember for how long, but you wake in tears at night. Big deal. u spend four nights a week now looking for your inner child. What you nna say when you find him? Suppose you don't like him or he doesn't like u? Suppose once you wake him up he won't go back to bed and wants to y up late watching TV? But you say there must be some reason why you feel this way. Big deal, that's the way we all feel. Big deal, what is it you wanna feel? You say you wanna get cured, you wanna turn off your head. Oh and you say it hurts, and you feel unsure. First you doubt yourself and then you doubt her. Big deal, that's the way we all feel. What is it you wanna feel? I don't think you wanna feel.

Mirrorball. You never knew the teenage me and you wouldn't believe the things you didn't see, some pretty, some ugly. And the lovely mirrorball reflected back them all - every triumph, every fight, under disco light. Come on girl, it's alright. Come on girl, it's alright now. Come on girl, it's gonna be alright now. Well I guess some boys adored me but the one I loved ignored me, and caused me in the end to murder my best friend. And though I got her letter, it never did get better, and I got out of my head. Then I joined a band instead. Some good times I remember - my birthday that September, we lay down on the lawn, and counted until dawn the stars that we lay under. And is he still, I wonder, the fairest of them all, mirror, mirrorball. Come on girl, it's too late. Come on girl, it's too late now. Let it all go. It's gonna be alright now. Oh it's never gonna be alright. But it's too late now. Let it all go. Cause it's never gonna be alright.

Good Cop Bad Cop. I don't wanna feel this way. I don't wanna feel this way - won't somebody take away this feeling. I'm looking at an open sky. It's like my roof has got no ceiling. It's wrong to feel this way. I know it's wrong, I know it's bad - to only see what isn't there, to want and want and never have. But you know there's more to me now, don't you? You'll always cover for me, won't you? And this used to look half-full. Now some days it looks half-empty. And some days it feels like nothing. It always used to feel like plenty. I don't wanna feel this way - won't somebody take away this feeling. You play good cop, I play bad cop. Still my roof has got no ceiling.

Exclusive Distributors:
Music Sales Limited
8/9 Frith Street, London W1V 5TZ, England.
Music Sales Pty Limited
120 Rothschild Avenue, Rosebery, NSW 2018, Australia.

Order No.AM939323
ISBN 0-7119-5991-9

Visit the Internet Music Shop at
http://www.musicsales.co.uk

Music arranged by Roger Day.
Music processed by Paul Ewers Music Design.
Book design by Michael Bell Design.

Printed in the United Kingdom by
Caligraving Limited, Thetford, Norfolk.

Before Today

Words & Music by Ben Watt.

G6
a thou - sand miles.
I don't want your at -
- ti - tude,
I don't want your things,
but
Bm7
A6
I don't want a phone that nev - er rings.
Gmaj7
I want your love,

Dmaj7
and I want it now,
Gmaj7
I want your love,
Dmaj7
and I want it now.
To Coda 𝄌 1.

2.
Gmaj7
My heart is that much hard - er now,
D13
that's what I thought be - fore
to - day,
my heart
Gmaj7
is that much hard - er now,

Bm9
and I thought that it would stay that way
A6
Gmaj7
be - fore to - day.
Dmaj7
Gmaj7
Be - fore to - day.

Verse 2:
I don't want your history,
I don't want that stuff,
I want you to shut your mouth,
That would be enough.
I don't care if you've been here before,
You don't understand,
Tonight I feel above the law,
I'm coming in to land.

Wrong

Music by Ben Watt. Words by Tracey Thorn.

B♭m7/E♭
E♭m
fr6
To Coda
-n't I?
I want-ed to know what {it / he} was like.
But I pushed you too far and you
start-ed lay-ing down the law till I
did-n't love you a-ny-more,
now you can pull a lit-tle bit.

G♭
A♭
fr4
Fm
And there's a lit - tle give
G♭
and take, and love will stretch a lit - tle bit
A♭sus4
fr4
Fm
G♭
but fin - ally it's gon - na break.
E♭m
fr6
B♭m7/E♭
fr6
E♭m
fr6
Wher - ev - er you go I will fol - low you 'cause I

B♭m7/E♭
E♭m
fr6
1.
2.
was wrong. Wher-ev-er you go I will fol-low you
'cause I was wrong. was wrong. And the ground's
gon - na swal-low you, I
was wrong. And the ground's gon - na swal-low you

E♭m
B♭m7/E♭
E♭m
fr6
I was wrong.
I
B♭m7/E♭
E♭m
B♭m7/E♭
D.%. al Coda
was wrong,
I was wrong,
Coda
B♭m7/E♭
G♭
A♭sus4
fr4
Now you can pull a lit - tle bit
Fm
G♭
and there's a lit - tle give and take and love will stretch a lit - tle bit

Verse 2:
So there we were both in that little house
Just hanging out.
You didn't know what you were about.
You turned to me as you were threading daisies on a chain
And you said "It's decision time again."
Now you can pull a little bit.

Single

Words & Music by Ben Watt and Tracey Thorn.

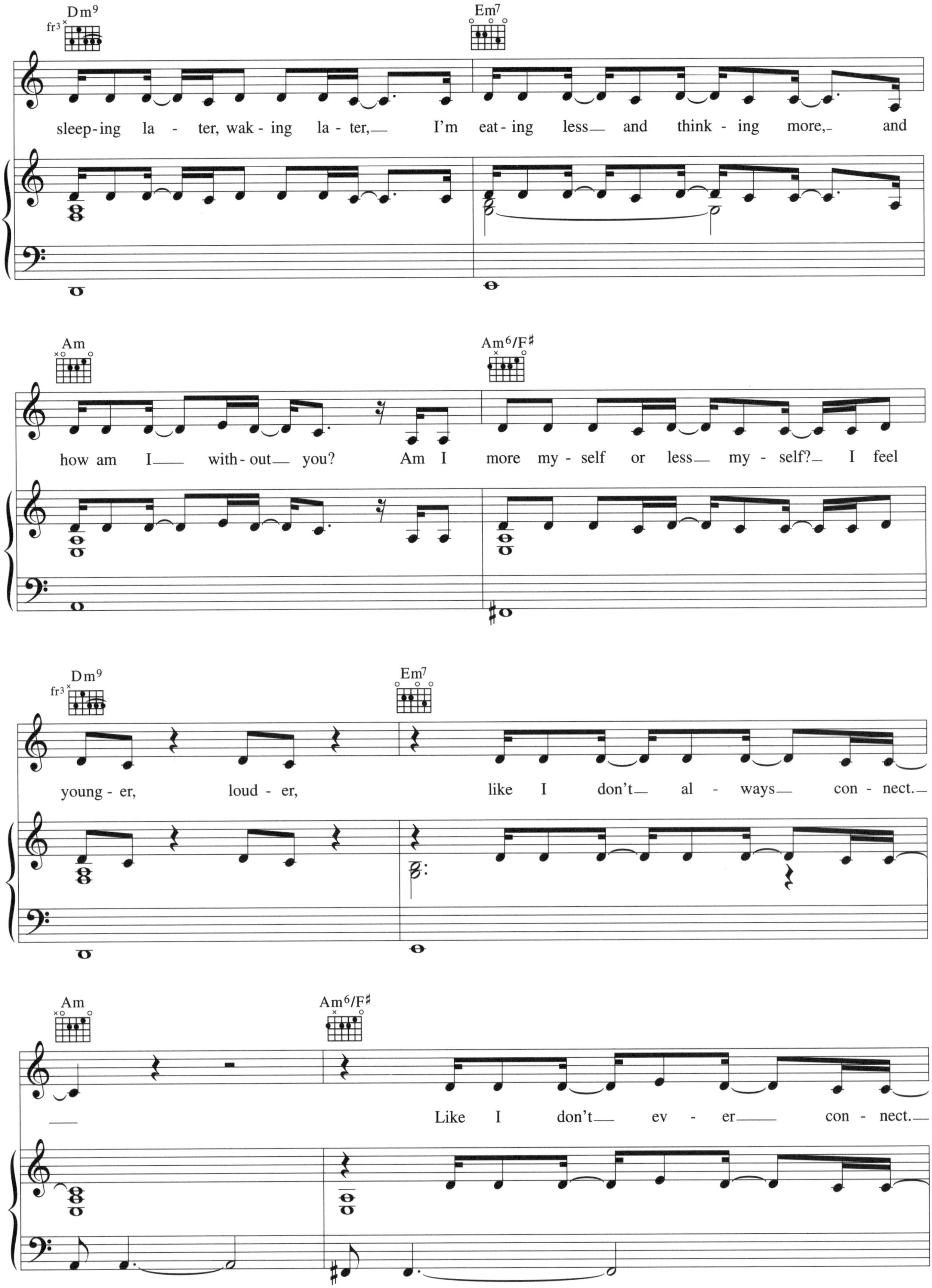
Dm9
fr3
Em7
sleep-ing la - ter, wak - ing la - ter, I'm eat - ing less and think - ing more, and
Am
Am6/F♯
how am I with - out you? Am I more my - self or less my - self? I feel
Dm9
fr3
Em7
young - er, loud - er, like I don't al - ways con - nect.
Am
Am6/F♯
Like I don't ev - er con - nect.

Dm9
Em7
Am
Do you like be-ing sin-gle,
Am6/F♯
Dm9
do you want me back,
do you want me back?
Em7
Am
Do I like be-ing sin-gle,
Am6/F♯
Dm9
1.
Em7
am I com-ing back,
am I com-ing back?
2. I

2.
Em7
Am
Do you want me back? Do you want me back?
Am6/F♯
Dm9
fr3
1.
Em7
Do you want me back? Do you want me back?
2.
Em7
Am
And now I know each
Am6/F♯
Dm9
fr3
1.
Em7
time I go, I don't real - ly know what I think I know. And

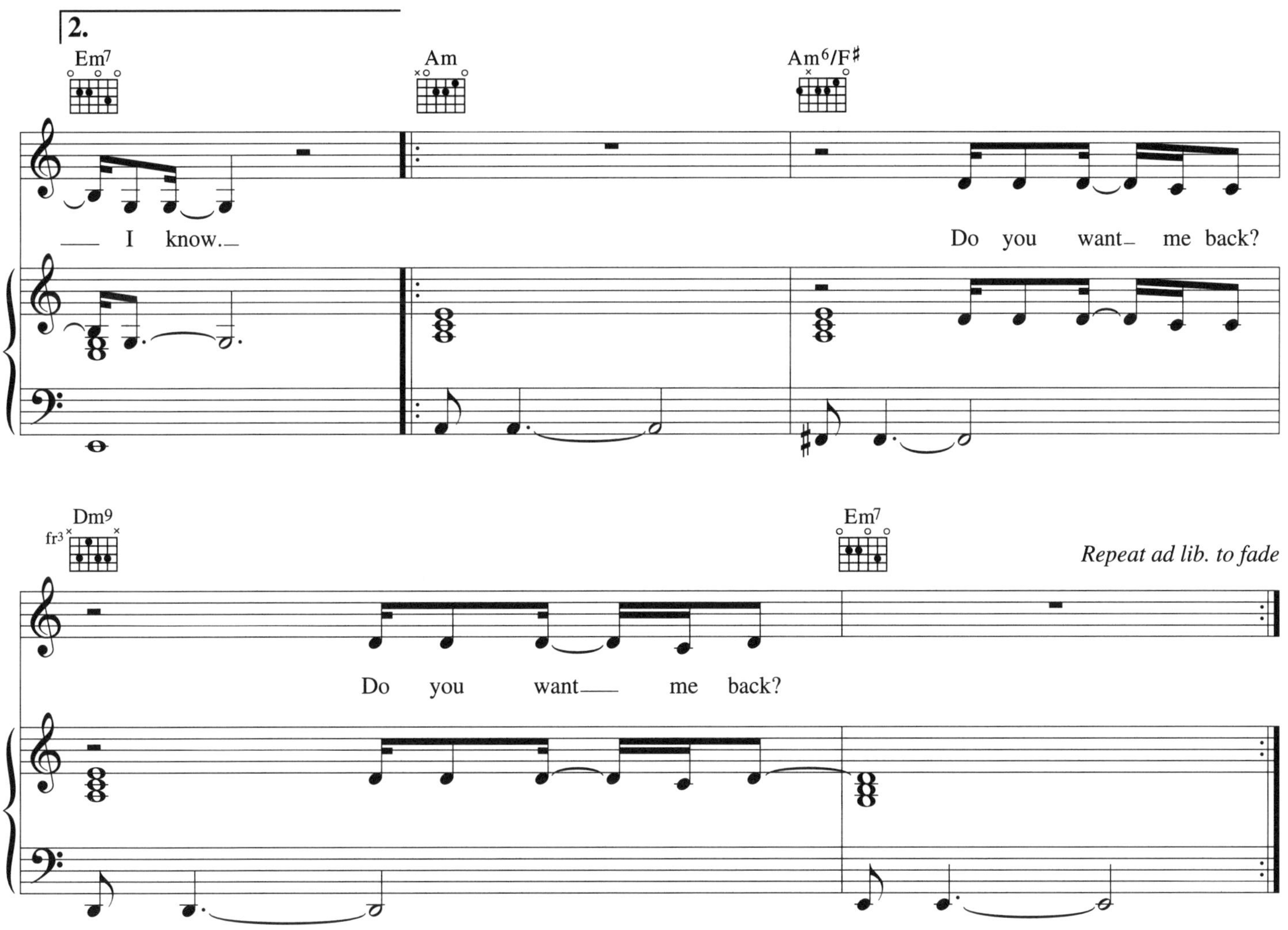

Verse 2:
I'll put my suitcase here for now,
I'll turn the TV to the bed,
But if no one calls and I don't speak all day
Do I disappear?
Look at me without you,
I'm quite proud of myself,
I feel reckless, clumsy,
Like I'm making a mistake,
A really big mistake.

The Heart Remains A Child

Words & Music by Tracey Thorn.

E♭
fr6
Fm11
fr8
nev - er have the same face twice, but I
D♭
fr4
al - ways know it's you and you're al - ways look-ing bet - ter than you
E♭
fr6
Fm11
fr8
real - ly do, than you
E♭
fr6
Fm11
fr8
real - ly do. And I

E♭ fr6
Fm11 fr8
E♭ fr6
walk a - round the whole next day,
feel-ing like I still got some-thing to say,
Fm11 fr8
D♭ fr4
but I don't know what it is
and I
E♭ fr6
Fm11 fr8
don't know how to reach you ev - en if I did,
ev - en
E♭ fr6
Fm11 fr8
B♭
if I did.
Do I wan-na hear that you for-give me?

B♭sus4
B♭
Fm7
Do I wan-na hear you're no good with - out me?
Cm7
fr3
B♭
And am I big e-nough to hear that you nev-er ev-en think a-bout me?
B♭sus4
B♭
E♭
fr6
Why should you ev - er think a - bout me?
1.
Fm11
fr8
E♭
fr6
Fm11
fr8
2. I

Verse 2:
I thought that I'd outgrow this kind of thing,
Tell me, aren't we supposed to mature or something?
I haven't found that yet,
Is this as grown-up as we ever get?
Maybe this is as good as it gets.

Years may go by
But I think the heart remains a child.
And the mind may grow wise
But the heart just sulks and it whines and remains a child.

Walking Wounded

Words & Music by Ben Watt & Spring Heel Jack.

C♯m9
-'ry bus is you and me and him and her, and
C♯m6
fr3
C♯m9
no - thing can re - place the us I knew.
C♯m6
fr3
C♯m9
no - thing can re - place
C♯m6
fr3
To Coda
the us I knew.

N.C.
7 bars rhythm
You know I'm nev - er gon - na let you go,
you know I'm nev - er gon - na let you go.
And now I know I had a choice
though you nev - er made it clear to me,
I thought you nev - er felt it

2º instrumental break
deep - ly.
Now I'm nev - er gon - na
let you go,
now I'm nev - er gon - na
let you go.
'Cause I could have
loved you for - ev - er,
I could have

1.
loved you for - ev - er.
What
C♯m9
C♯m6
fr3
do you want from me?
Are you try - ing to pun - ish me,
C♯m9
pun - ish me for lov - ing you,
C♯m6
fr3
C♯m9
pun - ish me for giv - ing to you,
pun - ish me for no -

2.
C♯m6
fr3
- thing I do, pun - ish me for no - thing,
C♯m9
C♯m6
fr3
pun - ish me for no - thing, no - thing?
2.
1.
3
I could have left you for ev - er. I could have
2.
C♯m9
C♯m6
fr3
What do you want from me? Are you try - ing to pun - ish me,

C♯m9
punish me for loving you,
C♯m6
punish me for giving to you,
C♯m9
punish me for nothing I do,
C♯m6
punish me for nothing,
C♯m9
punish me for nothing,
C♯m6
nothing?
D.%. al Coda

Coda
C♯m9
C♯m6
fr3
Out a-mongst the walk - ing wound-ed, ev-'ry face on ev - 'ry train is you and me and him and her, and some days I think I could go in - sane.

C♯m6
C♯m9
Some days I think I could go in - sane.
C♯m9
C♯m6
C♯m9
C♯m6
Repeat ad lib.

Flipside

Words & Music by Ben Watt.

E♭maj7/G
F/G
mo - tion - al bag - gage, hopes and fears seen some - how in a diff-'rent light, not as
E♭maj7/G
F/G
wrong, but not as right as they seemed be - fore. Was I diff-'rent then? Have I
E♭maj7/G
1.
changed? And will I change a - gain? 2. I'm
2, 3, 4.
F/G
E♭maj7/G

F/G
E♭maj7/G
I mean a lot, I mean a lit - tle, lit - tle.
F/G
E♭maj7/G
4º To Coda
I mean a lot, I mean a lit - tle, lit - tle.
F/G
E♭maj7/G
3º D.%. al Coda
3. I'm like a
Coda
F/G
E♭maj7/G
Pig - gie in the mid - dle.

Verse 2:
I'm thinking of a mental free-fall,
A partial total memory recall
Like what of the future, what of the past,
What of the present will last?
And say I did forget
And revert to the old ways, forget this hurt.
Am I better off or in reverse,
Untaught by experience and therefore worse?

Verse 3:
I'm like a coastline, a beach and spit:
Spurn Point and the rest of it.
The sea, the tide, the salt and foam.
I'm the blasted land,
The sand shifting, drifting out and back,
Then breached, drowned, defences down,
Rebuilt from this day on.
Or maybe not, maybe my moment's gone.

Verse 4:
Am I the same person I seemed to be?
Does all of this depress me?
I won't listen, I won't talk,
A weightless life, I moonwalk.
I mean a lot. I mean a little.
I'm supple, brittle, pig in the middle.
There's resilience inside my face,
But sometimes nothing. Deep space.

What I feel and what I fear
Is always here – my atmosphere.

Big Deal

Music by Ben Watt. Words by Tracey Thorn.

/B♭
Gm9
fr3
/F
it is - n't right,
and you don't re - mem - ber for how long,
Cadd9
/B♭
but you wake in tears at night.
Big
E♭maj7
Gm/F
deal,
big
E♭maj7
Gm/F
deal.

N.C.
You spend four nights a week now looking for your in - ner child.
Accompaniment tacet
rhythm only
What you gon - na say when you find him?
Suppose you don't like him, or he does - n't like you?
Suppose once you wake him up he won't go back to bed and wants to stay up late watch-ing T. V. but you

say there must be some rea - son why you feel this way.
Ebmaj7
Big deal,
1, 2, 3. that's
4. that's
Gm/F
the way we all feel.
the way I feel.
Ebmaj7
Big deal,
Big deal,
Gm/F
1, 3.
1. that's the way I feel.
2, 3. what is it you wanna feel? Big
4. what do you think she feels?

2.
To Coda
N.C.
You say you wan - na get cured,
Accompaniment tacet
rhythm only
you wan - na turn off your head.
Gm
fr3
You say you wan - na get cured,
Dm
C
you wan - na turn off your head.
Gm
fr3
Dm
C
Oh and you say it hurts and you feel

N.C.
un - sure.
First you doubt your - self and then
Accompaniment tacet
rhythm only
D.%. al Coda
Coda
E♭maj7
you doubt her.
Big
Gm/F
E♭maj7
2º only (I don't think you wan - na feel.)
Gm/F
Repeat ad lib.
1º only (What is it you wan - na feel?)

Mirrorball

Music by Ben Watt. Words by Tracey Thorn.

Gm7 F/A Cm7 B♭ Gm7 F/A
re-flect-ed back them all, ev-'ry tri-umph, ev-'ry fight, un-der dis-co light.
E♭ Gm7 F/A E♭ Gm7
Come on girl, it's al-right, come on girl,
F/A E♭ Gm7 F/A
it's al-right now, come on girl, it's gon-na be al-right now.
E♭ Gm7
1. F/A
2. F/A

F/G
E♭maj7
Some good times I re-mem-ber, my birth-day that Sep-tem-ber, we lay down on the lawn
Dm7
F/G
and count-ed un-til dawn, the stars that we lay un-der. And is he still, I won-der,
E♭maj7
F/A
Cm7
B♭
the fair-est of the all? Mir-ror, mir-ror-ball,
Gm7
F/A
Cm7
B♭
Gm7
F/A
mir-ror-ball.

Verse 2:
Well I guess some boys adored me
But the one I loved ignored me
And caused me in the end
To murder my best friend.
And though I got her letter,
It never did get better,
And I got out of my head.
Then I joined a band instead.

Good Cop Bad Cop

Music by Ben Watt. Words by Tracey Thorn.

Em7
F♯m7
feel this way.
Em7
F♯m7
Em9
D add9/F♯
1. I don't wan-na feel this way, won't some-bo-dy take a-way this
(Verses 2 & 3 see block lyric)
Em9
D add9/F♯
feel-ing.

Em9
Dadd9/F♯
I'm look - ing at an op - en sky, it's like my
To Coda
Em9
roof has got no ceil - ing.
Dadd9/F♯
Bm7
It's wrong to feel this way,
F♯m7
I know it's wrong, I know it's bad, to on - ly

Em7
F♯m7
see what is - n't there, to want and want and want and nev - er have.
Bm7
But you know there's more to me, now don't you? You'll
F♯m7
Em9
al - ways cov - er for me, won't you? Won't you?
1.
2.
D add9/F♯
F♯m7
Won't you?

Em9
Dadd9/F♯
Em9
Dadd9/F♯
D.𝄋. al Coda
⊕ Coda
Em9
- ing, still my
N.C.
roof has got no ceil - ing. I don't wan - na

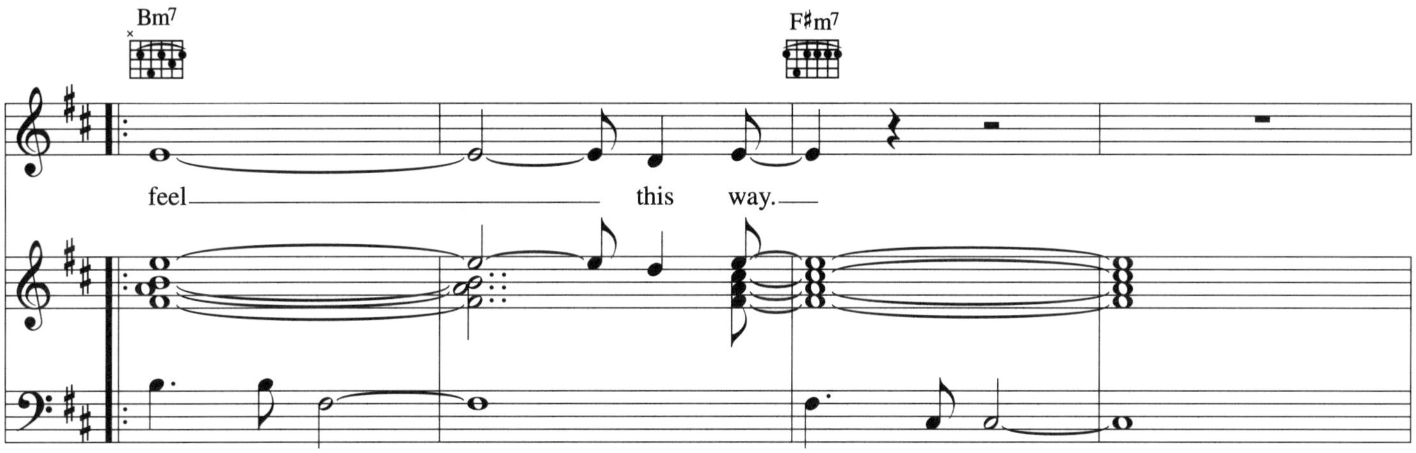

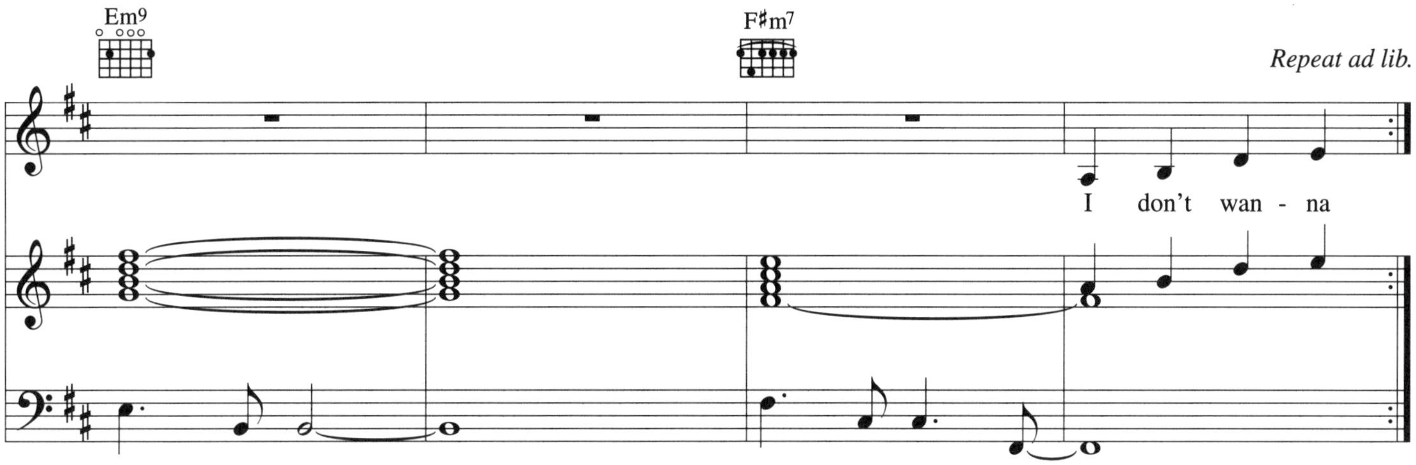

Verse 2:
And this used to look half full,
Now some days it looks half empty.
And some days it feels like nothing,
It always used to feel like plenty.

Verse 3:
I don't wanna feel this way,
Won't somebody take away this feeling?
You play good cop, I play bad cop.
Still my roof has got no ceiling.